MW00874507

UNDERSTANDING DREAMS & VISIONS

"Your Dream Book" - Dreams,
Visions and their Interpretations

By

Dr. Ricardo Vincent

ISBN: 1-4382-1235-6

Printed in the United States of America

CONTENTS

Introduction………………………………….. 4

1. Dreams and Visions…………………………….. 6

2. He Spoke to me in a dream…………………….. 8

3. God's Purpose for Dreams and Vision………… 14

4. Types of Dreams…………………………… 17

5. Dreams, Visions and their Interpretations……. 20

6. Interpretation caution…………………………... 24

7. Interpreting common dream symbolism………. 26

8. Dream symbolism of houses……………………. 29

9. Biblical symbols of colours……………………... 32

10. Biblical symbols of numbers………………….. 36

11. Some general symbolism from A-Z………….. 39

Introduction

Over the past decade scientists and psychologists have been studying dreams and are beginning to discover more and more about their seemly hidden secrets. Their research have produced useful insights into some of the subconscious activities that take place within our minds, and have provided some valuable technical information on dreams. This book however, focuses on the spiritual aspect of dreams and is hope to provide information that brings clarity and improves our understanding of them as a means of God communication with us.

Only recently, the Body of Christ has been becoming more and more aware of experiencing revelations given through dreams and visions. Now one can read more Christian books on the subject. Even on Christian Television it is becoming common hearing the Lord speaking to His servants and using this avenue to speak to His people.

The outpouring of the Holy Spirit and the subsequent manifestations of prophecy, dreams and vision are actually the fulfillment of biblical promises!

"And afterward, (in the last days Acts) I will pour out my Spirit on all people. Your sons and daughters will prophesy, your old men will dream dreams, your young men will see visions. Even on my servants, both men and women, I will pour out my Spirit in those days. and they shall prophesy"

Joel 2:28-29, Acts 2:17-18 NIV

Throughout Scriptures we see God communicating to people in dreams, in some cases he communicated directly by his servants and other times He used His prophets as His mouthpiece to communicate to Judges, kings, priest and nations. Dreams and visions were one of the most common means of communication God used in the Bible but it seem as if today it is ignored by most.

God wants to speak to people through dreams, especially his people, but we must understand this language so that He can give us instruction, direction, and reveal things about our selves, situations and even the future.

Chapter 1

Dreams and Visions

In the bible dreams are mentioned 122 times, vision 111 times. For an item to be mentioned so many times in the bible means it is of some significance.

DREAMS

"A succession (or series) of images or ideas, thoughts, emotions occurring during sleep".

(Webster's Dictionary)

"A series of thoughts, images, and sensations occurring in a person's mind during sleep"

(New Oxford American Dictionary)

One word used for dream in the bible Greek – "enupnion" – which is defined as "something seen in sleep".

VISION

"The act or power of perceiving abstract or invisible subjects as clearly as if they were visible objects"

(Webster's Dictionary)

The Greek word "chazon" means – divine revelation. Hebrew word is "chizzayown" which literally means revelation.

Dreams and visions are basically the same except that the dream occurs during period of sleep and the vision generally refers to images or revelations received in picture form while awake.

When there is a dream, it can originate either from our spirit or from God's Spirit - Issues from our own spirits seeking to be revealed or God through the Holy Spirit communicating to us His messages. There may also be cases where our dreams can be influenced by evil based on what we allow our selves to be exposed to.

With respect to the issues, these may reside in our sub-conscious mind, and God may communicate to our mind also while we are asleep. Then when we are awake we must be able to use our conscious mind to understand the dreams. Nevertheless, only God through the Holy Sprit can help discern and interpret dreams. That is, discern whether it is of the devil's influence, our soul or heart, a prophetic message from God or just a dream due to the activities of the day.

Chapter 2

He spoke to me
in a Dream

The first time I began to treat dreams with much significance was when I went to a church service in Miami and while walking through the book store I felt as if the Spirit of the Lord prompted me to take up a book on dreams, I did so, and look at it. As I thumb through the book the Holy Spirit took me straight to a specific chapter and my thumb just moved down the page as if by some strange impression and to one sentence and the statement was:

"God wants to speak to his people through dreams, but they are not listening".

The author continued by saying since it is the Holy Spirit who gives us the true meaning of dreams, when we have a dream we should pray and say:

"Lord give me the interpretation of this dream, and what you want me to understand from it".

Then the Holy Spirit will bring the interpretation and understanding to us. The author continues by saying, He will, if we ask.

So that evening when I returned to the place where I was staying in Miami, just before I went to bed I prayed:

"Father as I sleep tonight there are many things I want to know, so as I dream, Lord give me the interpretation of the dreams and what you want me to understand from them."

That night I dreamt I heard a voice saying:

"Come out into the road with a towel around you and stand before me", and in the dream as I did this a very tall man took me back into my bedroom and with a gun shot and made three holes over my bed head.

As I awoke I asked the Lord for the interpretation and understanding of this dream, and in my mind a thought came to me of Adam and Eve naked before the Lord. Then I felt as If the Lord was saying:

"Stand before me in the way, in the path I set for you, naked and exposed before me, open yourself before me in purity. Then I will send my angels to bring the blessing and I will bless you in three ways (the holes meant things to be filled) and the blessing will be complete"

(Three is the number of completion- three holes three things to bring to completion. The gun: the word of God. The bed, the place of rest)

I had another dream – and in the dream I can recall myself as a child and I was playing, holding a bed sheet and running with it between by legs, riding it like a horse. I then met an old man sitting on a stair-way who said:

"God has given the command for you to succeed, but you must observe the people"

As I awoke again, I understood what it meant. It was clear. This became exciting for me; so every day as I returned to my room from the University, I was anxious to sleep again to hear what the Lord would say. At that time I was studying a short course in Miami and was renting a room from a middle-aged Jamaican woman.

So, again I went to bed in the night and I dreamt I was standing in the sky, in the clouds, and the Lord Jesus was standing above me with his hands on my shoulders. He was dressed all in a white robe. I was looking at Jesus and myself. And as Jesus had His hands on my shoulders, he began to prophesy, and He prophesied and said:

"I will bless you in three main areas, I will bless you in your family, I will bless you in your education and I will bless you with wealth, but when I bless you be careful of pride".

As I received this dream, all the previous dreams connected together and I understood what the Lord was saying to me.

One of the things I have leant that as the Lord speaks to you whether in a dream or otherwise, you must write down what the Lord is saying so as he continues to speak, things will become clearer.

The time I had in Miami was also a time of teaching and stretching, as the Lord spoke to me in dreams. As he spoke it seem as if he also wanted to stretch me to help someone else.

One Thursday evening as I came from the University the landlady was waiting in the living room, all eager, as I came through the door, she burst into conversation as if there was some emergency, saying:

"Ricardo! I was waiting for you. I had a dream that has been bothering me and I was so anxious for you to arrive so that I can tell it to you".

As she said this, I shuddered a little, because I myself was just beginning to understand my own dreams.

She then put me to sit on the coach, sat next to me and began telling the dream. She said:

"I dreamt I was in a house, it seemed as a house I lived in when I was a child. While I was there, I saw a large honey bee with a crown coming down from the sky, as the bee came down there were gold dust falling from the bee. I did not want to get close to the bee so I took a cup and held my hand out the window to receive the gold dust from the bee. As I did this two police men came and took the bee away"

As my landlady spoke, she mentioned in the conversation that the house looked like a place where she had Bible Studies when she was a child. At the time she told this dream she was not attending any church.

"What could this mean?!" she prompted me.

As she said this, I remembered when Daniel was in Babylon with the three Hebrew boys and he was promoted

11

by the king for the meaning of the dreams, then he, Daniel went back and prayed with them...Understanding that God is the one that gives the interpretation to dreams.
I prayed quickly, under my breath.

"Lord, give me the interpretation of this dream and the understanding from it for this woman in Jesus name"

Then I said:

"The house represents a place, the bee with the crown seem to represent Jesus. Maybe, the Lord is saying to you that He want to you to be in that place where the word is ministered, as you were when you were a child. Maybe, he wants to send the blessing to you but you are afraid and staying afore off...Wanting the blessing, but not wanting to get close. If this continues it seems as if the Lord would remove himself far from you".

As I shared this with her, she acknowledged that she could have identified with what I said, and she felt this is what it really meant.

Friday of the same week as I came from the University the landlady met me again and had another dream to tell. As I sat with her I prayed again. In this dream she said:

"I saw in this dream two planes flying in the sky in opposite directions and as they flew against each other they crashed and gold dust fell from the sky and a year was written in the sky."

The Lord directed me to say:

"In this dream your path will cross with the Lord, and it seems as if the year written, is the year, you will not be afraid but you will fully give yourself to the Lord".

Several years later, the landlady called me from Miami to tell me that she was fully committed to the Lord and going to church. It was the year she saw in the dream, confirming what she saw.

"For God speaketh once, yea twice, yet man perceiveth not. In a dream, in a vision (revelation) of the night, when deep sleep falleth upon men, in slumbering upon the bed; Then he open the ears of men, and sealeth their instruction, that he may withdraw man from his purpose, and hide him from pride".

Job 33:14-18 (KJV)

Another version NIV says – "For God does speak – now one way, now another …. To ….warn man, turn him from wrong doing and keep him from pride"

Chapter 3

God's Purpose for Dreams & Visions

What is the purpose of dreams and vision? Should try to understand them? Well, many believe we should, and it is clear from scripture that God wants to communicate with individuals, churches, cities and nations. Dreams and visions are a means of God sending messages to people. Spiritual dreams and vision sent by God must be discerned, received and acted upon. We must learn to turn on our receiver so that we can benefit from them. God sends dreams and visions to us for a purpose, so we must seek to understand and benefit from that purpose. What does the scripture say about the purpose of dreams?

"I will bless the Lord, who hath given me counsel: my reins also instruct me in the night season."

Psalms 16:7 (NKJV)

"When a prophet of the Lord is among you, I will reveal myself to him in Visions, I will speak to him in dreams."

Numbers 12:6 (NKJV)

"For God speaketh once, yea twice, yet man perceiveth not. In a dream, in a vision (revelation) of the night, when deep sleep falleth upon men, in slumbering upon the bed; Then he open the ears of men, and sealeth their instruction, that he may withdraw man from his purpose, and hide him from pride".
                    Job 33:14-18 (KJV)

"For a dream comes through much activity"

Ecclesiastes 5:3 (NKJV)

The Hebrew word "activity" translates – concern. Dreams are often the products of natural anxieties, cares, and concerns. Sometimes they not have that much meaning behind them, but sometimes it can highlight what is on our minds.

The Purpose of Dreams then is:

- To give counsel to individuals or groups
- To instruct and give guidance
- To commune with God as he shares things to us about ourselves
- To save us from danger
- To save us from pride (to adjust ourselves in meekness)
- To reveal our calling/purpose or ministry gift to us.
- To bring correction, edification, and warning to the body of Christ.
- To reveal prophetically the future - giving us insight into what lies ahead.
- For the Holy Spirit to highlight some of the concerns of our heart

- To point out things about ourselves or what is in our heart to bring correction, warning, guidance, edification
- For God to reveal Himself to us
- It can also place a spirit of intercession upon us or give us a burden to pray for a particular person or event so that problems can be averted, (sometimes showing us things about others).

Note though, we may just dream based on the mere activities of the day. For instance, just after I finished college I was working for a retail car parts and car dealer company, I was in charge of the warehouse.

One day we had to offload two trucks with small boxes. We spent most of that evening throwing the boxes from the truck, to each other and then up the stairs. That evening when I went to sleep, all I dreamt about was "boxes flying in the air". This dream had no real meaning. It simply highlighted what was left in my mind due to the activity of the day.

Generally in our dreams and vision God wants to *give revelation, instruction and counsel.* When we over look our dreams though, there is so much we miss out on. To understand it and receive the messages from God is to save time and save us from pain and mishap and afford us much gain.

Chapter 4

Types of Dreams

Through scriptures we see that God has desired to communicate with his people. The use of dreams and visions were two of the most common ways God communicated to man in the Bible.

There are basically two different types of dreams:

1) Intrinsic Dreams: About 95%-98% or most of our dreams, for most of us of are intrinsic, meaning that they are talking about you and *what is going on in your heart*. There may be a few where the percentage of the intrinsic dreams, are at a lower percent, however, for most of us, most of the dream are intrinsic. These are dreams that reveal *what is going on in your life* and they deal with the issues of your own heart.

Please not this – your own heart. They deal with the mind, will and emotions. They are all about you. God is a personal God and He first wants to communicate to you and deal with you. For Him to highlight things about you in your life, for adjustment and fro Him to give you guidance to prepare you for the purpose He has for you.

In Genesis 37:1-11, Joseph had two dreams which fall into this particular category.

In this particular scripture Joseph dreamt of greatness. He had a symbolic dream of dominion and of his brothers and parents bowing down before him. The dream Joseph dreamt was about Joseph, himself. I believe with that dream came certain emotions and feelings that God wanted Joseph to be aware of, yet also God was also showing Joseph His intensions for him.

2) Extrinsic Dreams: About 2%-5% of our dreams are extrinsic. An extrinsic dream talks about *real outer situations instead of about you*. That is, situations that are not based on us as the topic but things that are external to us....Maybe the people around us; our environment; the city; the nation.

Extrinsic dreams sometimes reveal murders, airplane crashes, earthquakes, theft, or rapes before they actually happen. Pharaoh's dream about the fat and thin cows was an extrinsic dream speaking about the coming famine.

I personally believe that our intimacy with Jesus will have a great impact upon our ability to hear from the Lord through dreams, visions, prophecy and any other way the Lord wants to speak to us. *The greater the intimacy, the greater will be our level of ability to hear, see and receive from the Holy Spirit.*

Since most of the dreams we have then are about ourselves, it might be more prudent for us to first seek to see if the Lord is trying to tell us something about ourselves. And if so, ask the Holy Spirit what it is He is trying to tell us about our selves, and our heart.

The Spirit of the Lord speaks to our heart and it is our hearts that truly reveal our thoughts.

".. Son of man, receive into your heart all My words that I speak to you, and hear with your ears"

Ezekiel 3:10 (NKJV)

"Search me, oh God and know my heart; test me and know my anxious thoughts

Psalm 139:23 (NIV)

"….as a man thinketh in his heart so is he"

Proverbs 23:7

Our hearts when revealed in our dreams show us who we are or what we might be thinking.

If a dream is not about you and it is prophetic for your environment. As you walk close to God, you would know.

God created man with the ability to dream and see into the realm of the spirit.

Chapter 5

Dreams, Vision
and their Interpretations

Many time dreams have dual meanings. The Lord may show you in the dream something about yourself and yet, He may also show you something prophetic about those around you or things external. Joseph's dream although it was about himself, it was also prophetic about things to come.

How can we interpret the dreams that God gives to us? Do we need to go to the psychic down the street or should we go to the village obeah man (witch doctor). Though the Lord uses His servants the prophets, should we always run to them for interpretation or go to God himself?

"There is a God in heaven who reveals secrets, and He has made known to King Nebuchadnezzar what will be in the latter days."

Daniel 2:28 (NKJV)

If any of you lacks wisdom, let him ask of God, who gives to all liberally and without reproach, and it will be given to him.

James 1:5 (NKJV)

When we have a dream the first thing we must do is go to God in prayer.

There are cases where God may use his anointed servants – but God is the one through the Holy Spirit who gives the interpretations of dreams and visions.

Dream interpretation comes from the Spirit of God. As we ask the Holy Spirit to reveal the interpretation to us, He will be faithful to respond to our request. He will reveal the meanings behind the symbols. He will unveil the mysteries that He desires to make known unto us. He will give us eyes to see and ears to hear what His Spirit is speaking through our dreams and visions.

Are all Dreams & Visions from God?

NO!

Some are from our daily activities Ecc. 5:3
Some are from our own heart
Some are from the enemy (the Devil)
Some are prophetic revelations from God

But the Holy Spirit will make us aware – as we stay close to Him – and will reveal to us the enemy's strategy or what is in our heart. We must pray for discernment and practice discernment. The more time we spend reading and studying the word of God and communicating with Him, the easier it will be to discern where the dream is from and what it is about.

Understanding the Language

Dreams and Visions use a basic language of:

1. Symbolism
2. Numbers
3. Colours

Remember also, the dream may also have a dual meaning.

And whatever these represent one will find the relationship of these symbolism represented in the Bible. So, the more we read the bible and study it, the easier it will be for us to identify the symbolism and differentiate them.

For instance the Holy Spirit is referenced in the bible as water, dove and fire to name a few. Jesus is reference as the rock and living water. Dirty water is represented as sin. As we search the scripture we will also find that God is a God of specifics and many times He uses numbers to represent some significance.

As we allow the Holy Spirit to help us to interpret our dreams we should also understand that not all symbols mean the same thing to every individual. One person may dream of a bed and to him it may represent a period of rest, since in his experience he enjoys sleep, but for another it may represent a period of uneasiness, since in the other experience he never really sleep.

Do not be bound to the symbolism – let the Holy Spirit give the understanding as it relates to you or for you.

Once an interpretation comes, be sure to measure it by the Word of God.

Any revelation that does not agree with the Logos (written) Word of God should be rejected, however logical or relevant they may seem. If it passes this test, and you have responded in prayer, God may direct you to share it with a friend, counselor or pastor for confirmation or further insight.

You will not need to do this with every dream. That is, to share it with everyone.

In the following chapters are common dream symbolisms you can use as a reference, but as you refer to them note that for some of the same symbols there may be a negative interpretations or positive interpretations. The Holy Spirit will confirm with your spirit, the one that relates. There are cases though where some symbolism are always negative, or in most cases. For instance, frogs and darkness usually identified as demons or of the devil. There are some that most often are positive for instance, clear water, and pure white: the Holy Spirit.

Chapter 6

Interpretation Caution

All interpretations for your dreams or visions come from God and thus you should depend on him for its understanding. To seek to merely use symbolism and regimentally interpreting without the Holy Spirit is to go down a dangerous path. PLEASE do not use these symbols for your own dreams or anyone else's dreams with hard fast rules.

It should be stressed that it is to use both the *Word of God* and the *Holy Spirit's* total aid in using *symbols and types* when interpreting your dreams and the dreams of others. Another thing to consider is that different symbols may mean different things to different people.

Apply the oil of the Spirit, prayer and the Word of God in focus. If the Lord is talking to anyone about making a change, it is never His will or way to force or manipulate that person into making a change. To force, impose or manipulate anyone is tantamount to: *SORCERY OR WITCHCRAFT.*

Also, remember that some dreams are just dreams! The Bible says that we dream some dreams from much activity and many words. *(Ecc. 5: 3), so don't worry about it.*

How do you know if a dream is from God?

Through prayer, understanding of the Word of God, and relationship with the Lord and other believers as well as patience. Sometimes waiting to see if it comes to pass is the best answer. *(Habakkuk 2: 1-3)* NEVER make serious life decisions on a dream alone.

Make sure you get confirmation from others and from the Word. No man is an island! There is wisdom in the multitude of counselors. *(Prov. 11: 14)* Listen wisely to your brethren and never act on a whim or impulse. God will always confirm his word or message to you.

Chapter 7

Interpreting common Dream Symbolism

All of us would at some time or the other have dreams which include some of these symbolisms, and because these occur most often I refer to them as common dream symbolism.

Houses/buildings – Can represent a person's life, personality, the church or your spiritual state.

School - Can represent your spiritual state or maturity. It represents a state of teaching, or training and learning. Primary or elementary school: elementary level of Christian walk with God, a state of using spiritual milk Middle school or college: level reached with teaching and experience, stronger meat. University: a level of great experience and strong meat - A state of great responsibility.

People – May have several meanings – You may be prophetically dreaming about someone else or God may be showing you part of yourself that you see in someone else.

When dreaming about people, look at the outstanding personality traits of the individual, or what that person represents to you. How does the person make you feel? God may be pin pointing blind spots in you personality.

Crowds of People - This may represent public opinion. Look at what your response is to the crowd are within the dream. God may also be challenging you to come forth into a new era.

Flying – Flying to new heights may speak of new areas of anointing, levels or Giftings that God desire to move you into.

Clothing – The interpretation of this is based on the situation. Casual may be comfortable. Formal may be stiff or sophisticated. Naked – Being unprepared, open before God (if naked), fear of certain weaknesses or hidden matters exposed.

Animals – the animals represented would come from the dreamers individual experience. However snakes often represents trickery danger or tails being told. They may also represent wisdom (wise as a serpent)

Vehicles - gives indication of control. If the person is driving it can mean they are in control. If they are sitting in the back seat or passenger seat they have no influence in the direction or where things are going

Water:

<u>Waters:</u> Nations of the earth; restlessness; undercurrent; cross current; eternal life through Christ; Flow of the Holy Spirit; Word; spirit of man or enemy; unstable.

Water: Stagnant or muddy or polluted: Man's doctrines and ways; iniquity; haughty; spirit; unkind.

Water Troubled: Trouble; worry; sorrow; healing.

Water fountain: Spirit; words; spirit of man; Holy Spirit; salvation; source.

Water: Spirit.

Falling - Watch for a fall into sin; unsupported; loss of support; trial; succumb; backsliding.

Fire - Heat; burden; trial; persecution; passion; power; Spirit; gossip; revival; anger; envy; strife; desire; lust; affliction.

Chapter 8

Dream symbolism of buildings and houses

Since the key aspect of dreams is for God to deal with man either individually or collectively; and in the bible the body of man is referred as a house, so symbols "House and Buildings" was chosen to give more focus on. In the bible the spirit of man is "housed" in his body, the Church is the "House of God". In our personal house, there are varied aspects or compartment that the Holy Spirit will like to show us and deal with.

HOUSES or BUILDINGS

Represent a person's life, personality; the church or your spiritual state; one's own home; dwelling place; the temple. (Luke 11:24; 2 Sam 14:13-14, PS 119:54, Prov. 2:18)

Attic – That of the spirit; person's spirit; the mind, thought, attitude, memories. (Acts 1:12; 2:1-4)

Basement - Storage place; hidden, nature; soul; lust; depression; secret sin. (Jer. 38:6)

Bathroom – Repentance; confession; desire; cleansing; removing; expelling (Lev. 8:5-6; Ps 51:1-2, 7-10, Rev 21:26-27)

Bedroom – Rest; privacy; peace; good covenants and wrong covenants; uneasiness; intimacy; slumbering; laziness (PS. 4: 4; 139:8; Is. 28: 18-20; Heb.18:)

Childhood home – Something from the past that is of concern or an issue today for good or evil family (1 Tim 5: 4)

Den – Relaxed fellowship; too relaxed; notice where the focus is (Mark 2: 4-5)

Dining Room - The table of the Lord; communion with the Lord or with brethren; feeding on the Word. (Heb 4:13 1 Cor. 11:24)

Garage – Storage; ministry potential (Du. 28:8; Luk 12:18)

Kitchen – (Cafeteria/Restaurant): Preparation for teaching or preaching or the word; heart of the matter; hunger for the Word; motives; revealing (Heb 4:12, 1 Cor 11:24)

Living Room - Formal fellowship of church or place of fellowship with friends (Mark 2:4-5)

New Room – New birth; change for better or worse; fresh move of the Spirit (2 Cor. 5:17; 2 Cor. 5:1)

Old Room – Old man or ways; past; spiritual inheritance; religious traditions; natural inheritance (Gen 12:1; Jer. 6:16; Heb 2: 3)

Porch –Public place; revealed; exposed; outreach or evangelism (Mark 14:68; Acts 5:12)

Roof – The mind; logic; covering; shield of protection; heavenly revelation; ability to see all (Acts 10:9 Matt. 10:27)

Upstairs/Stairs – Upper room thought; prayer; going higher in the Spirit (Acts 1:13-14; 20:7-8)

Work Area - under development (Gen 2:15; Ps. 104:23)

Yard – Public part of life; in back could mean event that is behind or over or hidden (2 Sam. 17:18; Esther 1:5)

Library – Exploration into knowledge; knowledge stored up; abundance of word) 2 Tim. 2:15; James 3:13-18)

Chapter 9

Biblical symbols of colours

COLOURS

Black

Negative: Black is very seldom positive in a vision. Unless referring to a specific person, culture or race, the color black almost always speaks of darkness and the work of the enemy. Perhaps you will see a person in a dark room. All of these are negative. A dark cloud the work of the enemy ; judgment; famine; sin or evil.

Jeremiah 4:28 *"For this shall the earth mourn, and the heavens above be black: because I have spoken [it], I have purposed [it], and will not repent, neither will I turn back from it."* (GMR)

Ephesians 6:12 *"For we do not wrestle against flesh and blood, but against principalities, against authorities, against the rulers of the darkness of this world, against spiritual wickedness in high [places]".*

Blue

Blue is almost always a positive picture in dreams and visions – representing the Kingdom of heaven, heaven or heavenly visitation. Blue is a royal color in scripture. But, it can also speak of hurt or healing.

Proverbs 20:30 *"As the blueness of a bruise cleanses away evil: so [do] blow the rooms of the inward man."* (GMR)

Brown (or Tan)

Born again; without the spirit; repentance or turning from dead works (1 Pet. 1:24; Ps 37:2)

Gold

Gold has a positive meaning more often than a negative one. It speaks of royalty; wealth or favor. If a person has been given gold it means that God has given them authority.

Speaking of authority:

Daniel 5:29 *"Then commanded Belshazzar; and they clothed Daniel with scarlet, and [put] a chain of gold about his neck, and made a proclamation concerning him, that he should be the third ruler in the kingdom."* (GMR)

Speaking of royalty:

Psalms 45:13 *"The king's daughter [is] all glorious within: her clothing [is] of wrought gold."* (GMR)
Negatively it could also peak of greed/vanity - James 5:3, 1 Peter 3:3

Green

It can speak of things that are fresh and alive or immaturity/weakness, life – can be good or evil; provision; rest or peace. It can also speak of nourishment or favor. (Gen 9:3; Ps 23:2, 1 Pet. 1:24)

Orange

Warning; caution; Strong anointing as in the fire of God; purification; God's vengeance angels (Prov. 6:27; Acts 2:3, Zech 5:2, Is. 6: 5-7; Heb 1:7)

Purple

In scripture purple always has a positive connotation. It speaks of royalty of wealth and prosperity. In the Old Testament only the wealthy could afford purple clothing. So it was worn by kings and those of good repute. If you sold or imported purple cloth, then you were considered a wealthy merchant. Purple was also used in the tabernacle, representing the deity of the Lord. His royalty and Kingship.

Speaking of Royalty:

Esther 8:15 *"And Mordecai went out from the presence of the king in royal apparel of blue and white, and with a great crown of gold, and with a garment of fine linen and purple: and the city of Shushan rejoiced and was glad."* (GMR)

Red

Red can be both positive and negative. It can refer to blood; destruction and fire. Yet it can also speak of rubies; wealth and royalty (scarlet). It can also speak of forgiveness; cleanings; redemption or negative – sin; destruction. Rev 6:7, Ish 1:18

Silver

Silver speaks of redemption in scripture. To redeem (purchase) a slave would cost 30 pieces of silver. Silver also speaks of the wealth of the world. Also understanding knowledge, purity – Prov. 2:3-4......It can also speak of deceitfulness. Mth 26:15

White

Purity that dispels darkness, righteousness; God's majesty; redeemed, victory; of God (Rev: 1:14; 2:17; Is. 1:18; Dan. 7:9, John 4:35)

Yellow

Gold: Something good; honor; infirmity; sin (Ps. 68:13)

Chapter 10

Biblical symbols of numbers

NUMBERS

- Unity of God. Eph (4:1-6, John 10:30)

- Union, Division, Witnessing. (Gen 2:23-24, Rev 11:3)

- Resurrection, Devine Completeness and Perfection. (John 14:6, Rev 18:8)

- World, Earthly, Creative works. (Gen 1:14-19, Rev 4:6-8)

- Dive Grace, atonement, service (Eph 4:11, Ron 11:5-6)

- Weakness of man, sin, Flesh, Carnal (Rev 13:18, Dan 3:1-30)

– Spiritual Perfection, Completeness, Finish work. (Rev 10:7, Gen 7:2)

– New Birth, New Beginnings (Gen 17:12, Lev 23:26)

– Finality of judgment. (Gal 5:22-23)

– Testimony, Law, Responsibility (Rom. 8:38, 1 Cor. 6:9-10)

– Disorder, Judgment (Gen 10:15-18. Ex. 14:19-20)

- Is God's number of Government, Governmental perfection. (Matt 19:28, I Kings 4:7)

- Depravity, Rebellion (Mark 4:21-22, Gen. 14:4, Rom 1:29-31)

– Deliverance, Salvation (Ex. 12:6-7, Matt. 1:17)

– Rest (Lev 23. 6-7, 34-35, Est. 9:20-22)

- Love (1 Cor. 13:4-8)

- Victory (Gen. 7:11, 8:4)

- Bondage (Luke 13:16, Judges 3:14)

- Faith (Rom. 3:21, Ex 27:9-18)

– Redemption (Gen 21:38-41, Num 14:26-35)

– Exceeding sinfulness of sin (Tim 3:2-5)

- Light (Num 3:39)

– Death (Rom 1:28-32)

– The Priesthood, Elect (Rev. 4:4)

- Promise (Gal 4:28)

40 – Trials, probation, testing

50 – Pride

666 – Mark of the beast (Rev. 13:18)

Chapter 11

Some general symbolism from A-Z

A

Some general symbolic representations of dreams and visions from A-Z.

Adultery: Spiritual adultery; actual adultery; sexual sin *(Gal 5: 19-21; James 4: 4; Ecc. 7: 26; Ex. 20: 14; Ez. 23: 45)*

Airplane: Same as Vehicles – If you are driving your are in control (size is important)

Ankles: Relates to your foot, your faith, your walk.

Alligator: Same as snakes, crooked, distorted, ancient demon, principality (Is 27:151:9, 26:12-130)

Altar: See also Mountain, Table and Skyscrapers: Prayer; were made with hands in Old Testament; place where the bloodshed is purposefully conducted as a religious ritual; offering as a living sacrifice; Lamb of God, Jesus; table of the Lord. *(Ex. 27: 1; 2 Chron. 4: 1; 2 Sam. 24: 18-25; Gen. 8: 20; Heb. 13: 10; Ez. 41: 22)*

Anchor: Assurance of hope. *(Heb. 6: 19)*

Ankles: Belief that is not strong; God will heal; the believers faith. *(Ez. 47: 3; Acts 3: 7)*

Anoint: See also Balm: Set apart divine appointment in service *(James 5: 14; 2 Chron. 22: 7; 1 John 2: 20, 27; 2 Cor. 1: 21; Ex. 28: 41)*

Ant: Industrious, wisdom, preparation for future (Proverbs 30:35)

Antiques: Good or evil inherited from our ancestries; reflecting and recalling the past. *(Jer. 6: 16)*

Apples: Spiritual fruit; aroma; sweet allure; to be tempted to eat of the fruit of sin; a word fitly spoken; As the Apple of His Eye: God's care; security of the believer; the law. *(Zech 2; 8; Deut. 32: 10; Prov. 7: 2; 25: 11; Ps. 17: 8; Gal. 5: 22-23)*

Ark: Christ our security, strength, and deliverance; the Lord as totally man yet totally God; the Lord's seat of authority; man as God's dwelling place; intermediary or middleman; square container; baptism (Noah); heaven; atonement; holiness; God's law; understanding God's will; remembering His provision; covenant; testimony; authority. *(2 Chron. 6: 41; Ex 25: 16, 21; 16: 33, 34; 25: 22; 30: 6; 1 Sam. 6: 19; Lev. 16: 2, 14-17; 1 Peter 3: 20, 21; Heb. 9: 4; Num. 10: 33; 17: 10).*

Arm: Might; help; the Savior of the World; to be rescued; striker *(Ex. 6: 6; Duet. 4: 34; 33: 27; 7: 19; Ps. 89: 1, 10, 13, 21; 98: 1; 44: 3; 10: 15; Is. 30: 30; 40: 10; 63: 12)*

Armies: Godly or demonic might; armies could be led by God, Judges, Kings, and Commanders *(Heb. 2: 10; 7: 26; Eph. 6: 12-13; Jude 3, 4; James 4: 4; 1 John 2: 15-17; 1 Peter 5: 8, 9; 1 Tim. 6: 12; 2 Tim. 3: 8; 4: 7-18; Gal. 5: 17-21)*

Armor: See also Breastplate and Breast: Sacred gear for war; light; righteousness; the Bible and sword; shouldn't be of flesh. *(Rom. 13: 12; Eph. 6: 11-17; 2 Cor. 6: 7; 10: 4, 5)*

Arrows: See also Bow: The Word of the Lord's deliverance; lies and deceit; bitter words; God's Word unto affliction; quick and quiet judgments; gossip or deceitful speaking; fierce anguish; the commission of the Lord; the power of God; daily demonic attacks; intentions that are evil towards someone. *(Zech. 9:7-8; Is. 7: 16; Rom. 5: 3-4; Col. 2: 8; 1 Tim. 6: 20; Prov. 25: 18-19; Heb. 5: 8, 12-14; Ez. 18: 2; Ps. 11: 2; 45: 5; 64: 3; 76: 3; 91: 5; 119: 9; 127: 4; Jer. 9: 8; Job 6: 4; Du. 32: 23, 42)*

Ashes: Turning from sins; devastation. *(Gen; 18; 27; Ex. 9: 8; Is. 44; 20; 61: 3; Ps. 102: 9; Jer. 6: 26)*

Automobile: *Same as Vehicles*

Autumn: To turn from sin; transformation; concluding or termination of something. *(Jer. 8: 20; Is. 64: 6)*

Ax: Gospel; to motivate or give an admonishment to others by cutting away a non-truth; to preach. *(Prov. 27: 17; Matt. 3: 10)*

B

Baby: New Birth, barren woman, ministry in infancy, helpless, bay Christian, new thing, new move of God (1 Cor 3:! Gen 21:6, 1 Pet. 2:2, Heb 5:13)

Back: (as in direction): Returning to the past; behind you; over with; going backward; backsliding; hidden; unleavened cakes; or out of balance; cast behind someone's presence; casting sin behind. *(1 Kings 14: 9; Ex. 33: 23; Mark 8: 32-33; Phil. 3: 13-14)*

Backside: Past; something that is behind you; something that is over with; going backward; backsliding; to put or keep out of site; concealed from view: unleavened cakes; or out of balance; God's backside; cast behind someone's presence; casting sin behind you. *(1 Kings 14: 9; Ex. 33: 23; Gen. 22: 13; Josh. 8: 4; Mark 8: 32-33; Phil. 3: 13-14)*

Baking: Hospitality, God's provision, worship *(Gen. 25: 34; Lev. 26: 26; 23: 17)*

Balances: Integrity; judgment that is balanced with mercy or God's justice; man's tribulation; the smallness of man; something being shown as in balance; sickness. *(Job 31: 6; Ps. 62:9; Rev. 6:5; Dan. 5: 27; Is. 40: 12, 15)*

Balm: See also Anoint: A special anointing to heal. *(James 5: 14; 2 Chron. 22: 7; 1 John 2: 20, 27; 2 Cor. 1: 21; Ex. 28: 41)*

Bank: Storage, Reward in heaven, protected (John 2:15 Matt. 6:20, Luke 19:23*)*

Banner: *Also Flag:. (Ps. 20: 5; Ex. 17: 15; Song 2: 4; Jer. 50: 2)*

Baptism: Death and burial of the old man (nature) and his ways; *(Matt. 3: 9; Mark 10: 38; Rom. 6: 3-11; 1 Peter 3; Acts 2: 17-18; Acts 22: 16; Titus 3: 5; John 3: 3-6; 1 Cor. 12: 13; Gal. 3: 27-28)*

Banquet: *Blessings, abundance, systematic serving word of God (Prov 9:13-18)*

Barn: Church provision, place where wealth is stored, plenty (Prov 3:10, Matt. 3:13,13:30)

Basket: One basket equals one day; hiding good works; God provides; Judah and Israel's judgment. *(Matt. 5: 15; Amos 8: 1-3; Gen. 40: 16-19; Jer. 24: 1-10)*

Baptizing: Burial of the old lifestyle; total submersion in something; repentance; preparation for the coming Kingdom; death; burial; resurrection; inner conversion; overwhelmed by water or the Holy Spirit. *(Matt. 3: 9; Mark 10: 38; Rom. 6: 9; 1 Peter 3; Acts 2: 17-18)*

Barrenness: Unable to be productive for life of the Spirit; rejection; cursed; judgment; unfruitful; death of the Spirit; death of a ministry. *(1 Sam. 1; Gen. 11: 30; Deut. 28: 1-4, 15-18; Is. 5: 1-10)*

Bathing: Cleansing; repentance; totally clean; temptation; purification; ceremonial cleansing; Jewish ritual, before performing duties of the priesthood. *(Ez. 37: 9; Ex. 30: 19-31; Lev. 14: 8; 16: 4, 24; Gen. 2: 24: 32; John 13: 10; 20: 22; Mark 7: 2; 2 Sam. 11: 2, 3)*

Beam: God's might and power; supporting item or crutch; cry of vengeance. (Hab. 2: 11; Ps. 104: 3)

Beard: To esteem someone highly. *(Ps. 133: 2; Ezra 9: 3; Jer. 48: 37, 38; 2 Sam. 10: 4; 20: 9; 1 Sam. 21: 12, 13; Lev. 19: 27)*

Bed: *See also Bedroom*

Bells: The act of showing or displaying, in a tangible way, of the Spirit of God; sound that soothes; consecration. *(Ex. 28: 33, 34: 39: 25; 26; Zech. 14: 20; Is. 3: 16, 18)*

Binoculars: See also glasses or contacts: Prophetic vision; inability to focus: without ability to concentrate; a situation or person out of the proper focus. *(John 16: 13; 2 Corinthians 3: 13)*

Black: *See Colors.*

Blind: Lost; no proper understanding; in need of learning. (Matt. 15: 14; 23: 26; Rev. 3: 17; Lev. 19: 14; 2 Cor. 4: 4; 1 John 2: 11; Rom. 2: 19; Is. 43: 8; James 1: 23-24)

Bleeding: Spiritually dying, traumatize, to be in a state of disagreement with someone, someone speaking against someone else.

Blood transfusion: Saving grace; drastic change; rescued from sure death; conversion.

Body Odor: To be unexpected; unclean spirit; corruption of the flesh. *(James 4: 8; 2 Cor. 7: 1; Ecc. 10: 1)*

Book: The scriptures; learning or gaining understanding; revelation that can only come from God or man's wisdom; acquired information; instruction; important register; book of law; Book of Life; book of God's judgment; scroll: can be prophecy; eating is receiving the Word or whatever is written on what you are eating; genealogies; recorded miracles. *(Dan. 7: 10; Rev. 3: 5; 1: 11; 18: 8; 17: 8; 0: 12; Ez. 2: 9- 3: 3; Heb. 12: 23; Josh. 1: 8; 18: 9; Mal. 3: 16-18; 2 Kings 22: 8; Ez. 3: 1-3; Num. 21: 14; Gen. 23: 40-43; 5: 1)*

Bowl: Of full measure; worship in sanctuary; hide light under; note what it contains; completeness. *(Matt. 26: 23; Rev. 16: 1; Ex. 24: 6; Zech. 9: 14-17)*

Bracelet: *See also Jewelry:* Spirit of the world; commitment; confinement of the wrist which affects service. *(Gen. 24: 22; Ez. 16: 11; Is. 3: 19)*

Branches: Great triumph and conquest; churches; God's people; Israel; Christians, adversity; trees; vines; God's people filled with joy; abundance; budding branch can be new birth; salvation; blessing; ceremonial. *(Is. 11: 1; Rom. 11: 16, 21; Job 14: 7-9; 15: 32; John 15: 1- 6; Rev. 7: 9; Luke 22: 39-44; John 12: 13; Gen. 40: 10; Lev. 23: 40; Ez. : 10)*

Bread: God's Word; Christ our food that came down from heaven; God providing for His own; taught belief system; covenant; meat or essence; requirement for life; Last Supper; divine gift of God; life in Christ. *(John 6; 13: 18; Judges 7: 13-14; Mal. 1: 7; Matt. 4: 4; 15: 2-3, 6; 1 Cor. 5: 8; 11: 24; 2 Thess. 3: 8; Luke 1: 53; 12: 1; 14: 15; Ex. 5: 16; 16: 15)*

Breastplate: God as a shield of protection; righteousness. *(Eph. 6: 14; Is. 59: 17; 2 Chron. 18: 33)*

Brick: Stone that is man made; bondage; deeds of man; disobedience in setting up one's own plan. *(Is. 9: 8-21; 65: 3; Gen. 11: 3)*

Bridle: Self-constraint; not to be used on strong demonic forces (Leviathan) for they cannot be restrained in our own power; God's authority over flesh and tongue. *(Job 42: 13; James 1: 26; 3: 2, 3; Ps. 32: 9; Is. 30: 28; Titus 1: 11)*

Briers: To be disciplined; teaching that is false; sinful nature; a request turned down or suffering rejection; thorns; change in nature. *(Is. 5: 6; 32: 13; 55: 13; Mic. 7: 4; Heb. 6: 8)*

Brook: *See also Waters, Sea and River:* To make new or as if new again by refreshing; wisdom; prosperity; deception; protection. *(Job 6: 15; 20: 17; Prov. 18: 4; Ps. 110: 7; Is. 19: 6)*

Brown: *See Colors: also for Tan.*

Bruise: Hurt feelings or spirit; discipline; defeat for the devil; people in need of healing and restoration; injury. *(Lev. 22: 24; Prov. 20: 30; Matt. 12: 20; Is. 53: 10; Rom. 16: 20)*

Building: *See Places: also for Church Building.*

C

Candlestick: Those who carry the light of God; Jesus in the Church; the body of Christ universal and individually. *(Ex. 25: 31-35; Rev. 1: 12, 20; Zech. 4: 1, 2, 11)*

Cave: Hiding places of asylum and deliverance; wanderers; place where someone is buried; place of solitude where God speaks. *(1 Sam. 22: 1-2, 24; Heb. 11: 38; 1 Kings 18: 4, 13; 19: 5 Josh. 10: 16, 27)*

Chain: Captivity; to be spiritually oppressed; sin's bondage; disciple; satan's defeat. *(Rev. 20: 2; 2 Peter 2: 4; Jude 6; Lam. 3: 7; Rev. 20: 1; Jer. 40: 3, 4)*

Check: Money, treasure; the act of depending upon someone; belief in God or man's ways. *(Mark 4: 40; Heb. 11: 1; Luke 17: 5)*

Cheek: Trial; beauty; personal attack; victory; patience. *(Mic. 5: 1; Matt. 5: 39; Song 5: 13; Ps. 3: 7)*

Choking: Too much too fast; hatred; obstacle that obstructs the breath of God. *(Mark 4: 19)*

Christmas: New birth; pagan tradition; to merchandise God's gifts; spiritual gifts; performing humanitarian acts; to be full of joy. *(1 Cor. 14: 1; Luke 11: 13)*

Circumcision: Connection between people with a bond of agreement; cutting off carnal nature; free in the Spirit; regeneration; of Jewish bloodline; the born again Christian; cutting away of the law. *(Rom. 2: 29; Phil. 3: 3; Col. 2: 11; Jer. 4: 4; Du. 10: 16; 30: 6)*

Clapping: Praising; warfare; worship expression of thanksgiving and great joy. *(Ps. 47: 1; 98: 8; Ez. 25: 6; Is.*

47

55: 12)

Clay: Feebleness of carnal nature; kingdom that is not secure; distress through trial; fragile nature of the natural man; miracle; sealing. *(2 Sam. 12: 31; Is. 41: 25; 64: 8; Dan. 2: 33-35, 42; Ps. 40: 2; Job 38: 14; John 9: 6, 15)*

Clock: Time to make a change; time running out; not on time for something; an obstacle that causes one to not be on time; *time is significant in the Bible for:* the last days; coming of the Lord; day of salvation; time of bondage; captivity; wandering in the wilderness. *(Ecc. 3: 1-8, 17; Acts 14: 15-17; Ps. 89: 47; Eph. 5: 16; 2 Peter 3: 9, 15; 2 Cor. 6: 2; 2 Tim. 3: 1; 2 Peter 3: 3; Ex. 33: 5; 2 Kings 20: 9-11; 1 Kings 6: 1; Acts 7: 6; Du. 1: 3)*

Closet: Hidden or secret sin; confidential; prayer that is very personal; alone and obscure; good deeds and prayer done in secret (rewarded openly). *(Matt. 6: 6; Joel 2: 16)*

Clouds: *Dark clouds:* Judgment or attack from the enemy and can be the appearance of the Lord.

Clouds: *White clouds:* Glory of God.

Coat: Protective covering for shelter from the elements; a mantle of overseeing others or anointing; to cover someone's sin or to hide one's own sin. *(Matt. 5: 60; 1 Thess. 2: 5; 1 Peter 2: 16; Psalm 109: 17-29; 2 Kings 2: 14-15)*

Coat: *Clean:* To be covered in righteousness.

Coat: *If dirty:* To be clothed in unrighteousness or self righteousness.

Cord: *See also Rope or Chain:* To be tied to something that holds; sin; love; salvation. *(Ps. 2: 3; 118: 27; 129: 4; Jer. 38: 11; Ez. 27: 24; Job; 36: 8; Prov. 5: 22)*

Couch: *See also Bed:* Too relaxed; laziness; loss of concern; resting; privacy; peace; covenant (good or bad); intimacy; slumbering. *(Ps. 4: 4; 139: 8; Is. 28: 18-20; Heb. 18: 4)*

Court: Eliminated from His presence or entering into His presence; period of suffering; trial; judgment coming, conviction on a matter; acquittal on a matter; just or unjust system or judge; the accused having a voice; decisions are final; corruption unacceptable; contempt of not allowed. *(1 Cor: 6: 1; Is. 43: 12; Ps. 65: 4; 94: 20; 100: 4; Esther 4: 11; 5: 1, 2; Du. 17: 6-13; Rev. 11: 1-3; Ex. chapters 12-19; 27: 9)*

Crooked: Warped view or action; distorted spiritual picture; serpent; not on a straight path; a generation gone astray. *(Is. 42: 16; Phil. 2: 15; Du. 32: 5; Ecc. 1: 15; Job 26: 13; Ps. 25: 8; 125: 5; Prov. 2: 15)*

Crossroads: Christ crucified; options; job change; to have resolve. *(Luke 18: 22-23)*

Cymbals: Tremble and quake; praise; worship; to display insincere behavior or to make a lot of noise about love while exhibiting no action. *(1 Cor. 13: 1; 1 Chron. 13: 8; 15: 28, Ps. 150)*

Crawling: Unclean; humility; to have been cursed; disgraced; snake; idol worship. *(Gen. 3: 14; 1 Sam. 14: 11; Lev. 22: 5; Ez. 8: 10)*

Crying: Grief, sorrow, anguish, repentance, prayer; judgment, humility, sadness, sometimes tears of joy. It is important to note what the dreamer is feeling while shedding the tears. *(Mark 9: 24; Ps. 34: 6)*

D

Dancing: Worship, spiritual sacrifice, joy, rejoice, idolatry, seduction, whirling, evil and sensual, victory, return of a son. *(Ps. 30: 11; 149: 3; 1 Sam. 18: 6, 7; Ex. 32: 19; 2 Sam. 6: 14, 16; Luke 15: 21-25; Matt. 11: 16-17; 14: 6; Judges 11: 34; Lam. 5: 15)*

Drawing: See also Painting: Covering, regenerate, remodel, renovate, love. *(1 Peter 4: 8; Matt. 23: 27; Titus 3: 5; Acts 18: 24)*

Dreaming: To dream that you are dreaming, a message within a message, instruction from God; revelation of God's will or the future; keep dreamer from some evil; a vision; a deep Spiritual truth. *(Gen. 40: 8; 20: 3; 28: 11-22; 37: 5-10; Matt. 1: 20; 27: 13; 19; Judges 7: 13-15)*

Drinking: Consuming upon own lust; fellowship; as in wine and communion; whether good or evil; drinking in the Holy Spirit; under the power of sorrow; affliction; overcome; idolatry; under a strong delusion; from the blood of the saints (persecution); cup of the crucified life. *(Acts 2: 13; Jer. 2: 18; 51: 7; Is. 29: 9-11; 63: 6; Ez. 23: 33; Rev. 14: 8-10; 17: 2, 6; Du. 32: 4; 7; Zech. 9: 15-17)*

Drowning: Overcome; self-pity; depression; grief; being in debt; suffering; temptation; to backslid. *(1 Tim. 6: 9;*

Rev. 12: 15-16; Is. 61: 3)

Dam: Restriction to the power and flow of God, or of the opposition of the enemy; barrier; source of might. *(Josh. 3: 16)*

Darkness: Unfamiliarity; the darkness or shadows seen by a blind person; deep grief; turmoil; spiritual or supernatural darkness; eternal darkness; hell; death; immorality; to be innocently ignorant of truth; afflictions; to be in sin's way. *(Matt. 8: 12; 22: 13; 27: 45; Acts 13: 8-11; Ps. 112: 4; Eph. 5: 11; Rom. 13: 12; 1 John 2: 8-11; Job 10: 21, 22)*

Daytime: Truth; evil exposed; time of good deeds; present age; eternity; a time for the prophetic; the return of the Lord; believer's; the present time; space; light; length of productive time; understanding being illuminated. *(Dan. 7: 9, 13; 12: 11; Ps. 90: 4; Rev. 2: 10; Heb. 1: 2; Is. 22: 5; Gen. 2: 4; John 9: 4; 2 Peter 3: 8; 1 Thess. 5: 2-8; 1 Cor. 3: 13; Eph. 5: 13)*

Deaf: Not paying attention because of turning a "deaf" ear; spiritually, mentally or physically enabled; long-suffering. *(Matt. 11: 5; Is. 29: 18; Ps. 38: 13; 58: 4; 42: 18, 19)*

Desert: Forsaken; seclusion; destitute; ineffective and unable to produce fruit; hopeless; wilderness; temptation; supernatural provision. *(Jer. 17: 6; 50: 12, 39; Is. 21: 1; 27: 10; 33: 9; 40: 3; Ps. 107: 4-5)*

Diamond: Something valuable and precious; gift of the Spirit; stubbornness; cruel; inability to change; everlasting; radiant; majesty. *(Zec. 7: 12; Ez. 3: 8-9; 28: 13; Prov. 17: 8; Zech. 7: 12; Jer. 17: 1)*

Disease: Catastrophe; judgment; attack from satan; trial as part of life. *(2 Cor. 112: 7-10; John 9: 1-3; Luke 13: 16; Job 2: 7; 2 Chron. 21: 12-19; 2 Kings 5: 25-27)*

Ditch: Tradition or ritual that leads to a trap; sin; following the blind; fleshly desires. *(Prov. 23: 27; Matt. 15: 14; Luke 6: 39; 2 Kings 3: 16-20; Ps. 7: 15)*

Door: Jesus; opening; to be given admittance; possibility of danger or good; opening of the mouth to speak edification or idle words. *(Hos. 2: 15; 1 Cor. 16: 9; 2 Cor. 2: 12; Col. 4: 3; John 10: 7, 9; Rev. 3: 8, 20; 4: 1; Ps. 141: 3)*

Down: Spiritual decline; backslide; falling away; humility; prostration. *(Du. 22: 8; 2 Cor. 12: 18; Ps. 37: 31)*

Drink: fellowship; famine; pleasures of marriage; to have an alliance that is ungodly; receiving God's blessings; communion; under the influence of an evil spirit or unruly flesh; taking in the Holy Spirit or an evil spirit; unhappiness. *(1 Cor. 10: 4, 21; 12: 13; John 4: 13-14; Prov. 5: 15-19; Rev. 14: 8-10; Mark 16: 18; 2 Kings 18: 27; Rom. 12: 20; Eph. 5: 18; Matt. 26: 42; Zech. 9: 15-17; Is. 51: 22-23)*

Drugs: *See also Drunk and Drinking:* Additive personality; gossip; contention; witchcraft as a work of the flesh; controlling; imposing the will of one over another; actual drug problem. *(1 Sam. 15: 23; Prov. 17: 22; Gal. 3: 1)*

Drunk: Intoxicated in the natural, or with wrong beliefs, or in the Spirit; affliction; under the influence of an evil spirit or unruly flesh; overcome; under the power of sorrow; under a strong delusion; from the blood of the saints (persecution); idolatry. *(Acts 2: 13; Jer. 51: 7; 2 Kings 18:*

27; Is. 51: 22-23; 63: 6; Prov. 5: 15-19; Ez. 23: 33; Rev. 17: 2; Du. 32: 42)

Dust: Shame; mockery; descendants; to be cursed or under a curse; death; shortcomings of man; flesh of man. *(Matt. 10: 4; Acts 13: 51; 22: 33; 1 Sam. 2: 8; 2 Sam. 16: 3; Is. 47: 1)*

E

Eating: See also Dining Room under House: Experience; covenant; agreement; partake; friendship; fellowship; devour; consume; consuming wisdom; meditation; digesting the Word of God; forbidden fruit; no blood; no unclean foods; gluttony; adoption; must work to eat; respect a brother when choosing food. *(Gen. 2: 16-17; Ex. 24: 11; Jer. 15: 16; 52: 33-34; Rev. 10: 9-10; Luke 13: 26; 22: 15-20; Du. 14: 1-29; 20: 14; Matt. 11: 18; Ez. 3: 1-3; John 4: 34; 13: 18; Acts 14: 22; 15: 19-20; Phil. 2: 12; 3: 19; Josh. 9: 14-15; Prov. 30: 20; Rom. 14: 1-23; 2 Thess. 3: 7-10)*

Ear: Hearing spiritual things that either build up or tear down; lack of hearing not good. *(Prov. 2: 2; 4: 20; 17: 4; 28: 9; Is. 1: 10; 1 Cor. 2: 9; Job 13: 1)*

East: Light; God's glory; arising; birth; first; anticipate; false religion; Cherubim; the sun rising; East Gate: in the temple area; East Wind: brings judgment; causes springs and fountains to dry up; causes ships and vegetation to dry up; beginning. *(Ps. 103: 12; Rev. 7: 21; 16: 12; Ge. 3: 24; 11: 12; 41: 6, 23, 27; Ez. 10: 19; 11: 1; 17: 10; 27: 25-27; 43: 1, 2; Is. 27: 8; Ho. 13: 15)*

Echo: Accusation spoken over and over; many opinions vocalized; to imitate in order to make fun of; meaningless prayer. *(Luke 23: 21; Matt. 6: 7)*

Egg: Vulnerable; seed; promise that Abraham received of being many nations; promise of an Isaac or a work of the Spirit of God; the possibility for growth and development in any manner; revelation. *(Luke 11: 12; 1 Tim. 4: 15)*

Egypt: The world and being of the world; blackness; persecution; come out of; superstitious; ambitious; unprofitable; lowly kingdom; will be destroyed. *(Is. 19: 3, 19-25; 30: 1-7; 36: 6; Jer. 46: 8-9; Gen. 15: 13; Ez. 29: 14-15; 30: 24-25; Matt. 2: 15)*

Electricity: Spiritual power of God or demonic; potential for God, or for evil; destruction; flow. *(Matt. 9: 8; Luke 10: 19; 22: 53)*

Elevator: Jesus returning from the heavens to earth; symbolic of victory; Jesus being lifted up on the cross; wisdom that comes from above; Beatitudes in the Sermon on the Mount. *If going up:* moving up into the realm where God dwells. *(Du. 22: 8; 2 Cor. 12: 18; Ps. 37: 31; Acts 1: 13-14; 20: 7-8; Ps. 103: 11; 1 Sam. 9: 12-14; Matt 5; 1 Kings 12: 31; 18; John 3: 7; James 3: 15, 17; Heb. 1: 3; 1 Thess. 4: 13-18)*

Explosion: Violent pressure being quickly released in a destructive way from emotional unrest; expansion or increase; quick work; devastating change. *(Ps. 11: 6; Du. 32: 22; Is. 48: 3)*

Eyes: Longing for God; unnatural desire for someone else's possession; intense desire; lust of the eye; the window to the heart; depth and maturity of spiritual things; ability to see beyond the norm; knowledge and understanding revealed; evil desires; spiritual dullness; being of the world; illumination and future glory; unworthiness for service; the state of one's moral behavior. *(Num. 24: 3; Rev. 1: 7; Judges 17: 6; 7: 17; Is. 29: 18; 33: 17; 42: 6-7; 52: 8; 2 Chron. 16: 9; Ps. 19: 8; 32: 8; 33: 18; Hab. 1: 13; 1 Sam. 18: 9; 2 Peter 2: 14; 1 John 2: 16; Eph. 1: 18; 6: 6; 1 Cor. 2: 9; Is. 52: 8; Jer. 9: 1; Matt. 5: 38; 6: 22, 23; 7: 3-5; 13: 15; Mark 8: 17-18)*

F

Face: Expression shows feelings; something portrayed; the spirit of man; revealed true through a face; face reveals the nature of someone; notice expression and mood; nature; *to hide:* disapproval: *to fall on:* worship; *to cover:* mourning; *to turn from:* rejection; *setting toward something:* determination. *(Gen. 1: 26-29; 3: 19; 17: 3; Prov. 21: 29; Rev. 4: 7; 10: 1; 22: 4; 2 Chron. 30: 9; 2 Kings 12: 17; 2 Sam. 19: 4; Du. 31: 17-18)*

Fan: Work of the flesh to imitate a cool breeze of the Spirit; division of the impure and pure; *Christ's fan in one's hand:* purging His threshing floor.*(Matt. 3: 12; Luke 3: 17; Is. 441: 16; Jer. 15: 5)*

Feathers: Protective spiritual covering; weightless; God's protection. *(Ez. 17: 3, 7; Ps. 91: 4; Matt. 23: 37; Dan. 4: 33)*

Fence: Freedom of the Spirit endangered by being encircled and surrounded; self-control; security; tradition that hinders; lines or areas separating us from doing God's will or from sin (a wall or fence keeps things out, both righteous things and evil things); partition; obstruction; safety area; belief systems; to be held back or restrained. *(Is. 5: 2; Ps. 62: 3; Num. 32: 17; Gen. 11: 6; Jer. 15: 20)*

Finger: *Pointed finger:* could be finger of God to accuse or direct; perverse heart; teach or give instruction; clear-sightedness in seeing evil or good; specific convicted heart; deeds, encouragement; God's mighty work; authority of God. *(Luke 11: 20; Dan. 5: 5; Ex. 8: 19; 29: 12; 31: 18; Prov. 6: 13; Is. 2: 8; 58: 9; Du. 9: 10)*

Fire: Heat; burden; trial; persecution; words or the tongue; burning fervency; emotion, longing, aching and craving; power; Holy Spirit; angels; Christ Jesus; evil speaking; renewal in the hearts of men; anger to violence; envy; discord; affliction; removal of impurities. *(1 Sam. 17: 40; Matt. 3: 11; 14: 17-21; 25: 2, 15-20; Luke 12: 49-53; 19: 18-19; Jer. 5: 14; 23: 29; Ex. 22: 6; Prov. 6: 27, 28; 26: 20; James 3: 5-6; 1 Cor. 7: 9; Ps. 79: 5; 89: 46; Zech. 2: 5; Is. 43: 2; 6: 5-7; Heb. 1: 7; 12: 39; Mal. 3: 2; Acts 2: 3; Song 8: 6; Rev. 19: 20; 20: 10, 14; 21: 8)*

Flood: Judgment on those who use whatever power they have to inflict violence on others; sin judged; overcome; to be overcome and unable to recover; enticed to sin and fall; overcoming sadness and grief; great destruction and trouble; worldly powers that are hostile; invading army; trial; persecution. *(Ps. 29: 10; 32: 6; 93: 3; Jer. 46: 7, 8; Dan. 9: 26; Matt. 7: 25-27; Rev. 12: 15-16; Is. 28: 15-17; 43: 2; 59: 19; Gen. 6: 17)*

Flowers: Man's glory of the flesh that is passing away; an offering; glory of God; the Holy people and land of God,

Israel. *(1 Peter 1: 24; Song 2: 1; James 1: 10, 11; Is. 28: 1; 40: 1-3; Job 14: 2; Esther; Hosea 14: 5; Song 2: 1-2; 5: 13; 7: 2)*

Fog: Concerns or mindsets that are darkened by fog or clouds; something concealed; vagueness. *(James 4: 14; Hosea 6: 4; Job 10: 15)*

Forest: Nations; forewarning of trial; showing a place of danger and darkness where one can be easily lost and harmed; person lost; confusion and lack of direction; nations of the world or church; a grove. *Hos. 2: 12; Jer. 12: 8; 21: 4, 14; 26: 18; Is. 10: 18-19; 44: 23; Ez. 15: 1-6; 20: 46-49; Ps. 104: 20; 107: 4-5)*

Front: Future, now, in the presence of, a prophecy of future events, impending, visible, out front. *(Gen. 6: 11; Rev. 1: 19)*

Furnace: The origin of heat, the heart, rage, zeal, anger, trouble through great, heated and painful experiences, retaliation, the final wrath of God. *(Gen. 19: 28; Du. 4: 20; Prov. 17: 3; 1 Kings 8: 51; Isa. 31: 9; 48: 10; Ps. 12: 6; 39: 3)*

Falling: Watch for a fall into sin, unsupported, loss of support, trial, succumb, separation from God, backsliding, born in sin, power of God to change, to be depraved, evil heart, corrupted, bondage to satan or/and sin, spiritually blind, Falling and getting up: A righteous man seven times. *(John 3: 6; 3: 16; Titus 1: 15; Eph. 4: 18; Heb. 2: 14, 15; Matt. 15: 19; Rom. 3: 12-16; 6: 19; Col. 2: 13; James 1: 2; Prov. 16: 18; 22: 14; 11: 28; 24: 16; Micah 7: 8)*

Feeding: Also being Fed: To be supplied in a spiritual or supernatural way; narcissism, works that are righteous, basic teaching, change in basic traits of one's nature, to become impure in character. *(Rev. 12: 6; 1 Cor. 3: 2; Hos. 12: 1; Matt. 25: 37; Is. 11: 7; Ps. 49: 14)*

Flying: Spirit, minister, prophet, Holy Spirit, defense and shelter. *(Mal. 4: 2; Is. 40: 31; Ex. 19: 4; Ps. 91: 4)*

G

Garbage: The pit of hell, abandoned things, pure corruption, reprobate or unclean, unclean spirit, departure from all that is Godly. *(1 Cor. 9: 27; Mark 9: 47)*

Garden: Increase, work, ministry of the body of Christ collectively, euphoric paradise, fruitfulness, prospering ministry, field of labor, fertile ground. *(Gen. 2: 8-10; 4: 2-3; Is. 51: 3; 58: 11; Jer. 2: 21; 1 Tim. 4:14-15)*

Gardening: Increase, work, ministry, church, pleasant, fruitfulness, prospering, pastime, field of labor. *(Gen. 2: 8-10; 4: 2-3; Is. 51: 3; 58: 11; Jer. 2: 21; 1 Tim. 4:14-15)*

Gasoline: Energy; strife that is kindled by words; faith filled; *(Jude 1: 9; Prov. 26: 20-21; 24: 28; James 3: 14-15; Matt. 24: 4)*

Gate: *See also Door:* Entering into; domination; dominion; power of authority; satanic power; righteousness; death; heaven; salvation; thanksgiving; entering the presence of God; gates open up to: cities; prisons; sanctuaries; graves. *(Gen. 19: 1; 22: 17; 24: 60; Hos. 2: 15; Ex. 32: 26-27; Heb. 13: 12; 1 Cor. 16: 9; 2 Cor. 2: 12; Col. 4: 3; Matt.*

16: 18; 27: 60; John 10: 7, 9; Rev. 4: 1; 3: 8, 20; Ps. 24: 7; 100: 4; 107: 16; 122: 2; 141: 3; Judges 16: 3; Ez. 44: 1-2; Acts 12: 5)

Girdle: *Also to Gird up:* Vigor, might and potency for battle; a belt. *(Ps. 18: 39; 30: 11; 65: 6; Is. 22: 21; 45: 5; Ex. 28: 4, 39; 1 Sam. 18: 4; John 13: 3-4; Luke 12: 35; Job 12: 18; 30: 11; Eph. 6: 14; 1 Peter 1: 13)*

Gloves: Also see Hands: Protective covering for service; safety in the work of the ministry. *(Ps. 24: 3-4)*

Grapes: Fruit of the Spirit; His Word in seed form; The Lord's vow to us; coming wrath of God; Word of God; abiding in the vine who is Jesus. *(Song 7: 7; Matt. 7: 16; Rev. 14: 18; Num. 6: 3; 13: 20-34; Gen. 40: 10-11; 49: 11; Ez. 18: 2; Gal. 5: 22-23; Matt. 20: 1-6; Hos. 14: 7; John 15: 1-2, 6; Is. 5: 1-7; Ps. 128: 3; 1 Kings 4: 25)*

Graveyard (and Grave): Curse of the law; behaving sanctimonious; death; demonic influence; resurrection life of God, resurrected from grave. *(Matt. 23: 27; Luke 11: 24)*

Guns: *See also Arrows:* Spoken words that wound; to bring a charge against the elect; malicious and venomous speaking; power of words in prayer; dominion through speaking the Word of God. *(Ps. 64: 4; Luke 11: 21-22; Acts 19: 13, 15-16*

H-P

Ironing: Correction; change; sanctification; exhortation; instruction in righteousness; God's discipline; repentance;

working out problem relationships; reconciliation; pressure from trials. *(Eph. 5: 2)*

Kiss: Agreement; covenant; enticement; betrayal; covenant breaker; deception; seduction; friend. *(Ps. 2: 12; Prov. 7: 10, 22-23, 27; 27: 6; Luke 22: 48; 2 Sam. 20: 9-10)*

Kneeling: Submission, worship, prayer, total surrender. *(Dan. 6: 10; Ps. 95: 6; Mark 10: 17; Acts 20: 36)*

Laughing: Rejoicing; joy of worship and walk with God; sarcasm. *(Ps. 59: 8; Job 5: 20; Gen. 18: 11-15; 2 Chron. 30: 10; Prov. 1: 26; 2: 4; 22: 7; 37: 13; 80: 6; 126: 2, 3)*

Lifting Hands: Worship and adoration; praise; total surrender. *(Ps. 141: 2; Rev. 10: 5; 1 Tim. 2: 8; Neh. 8: 6)*

Limping or Unable to Walk: Shortcomings; weakness; inconsistency; not fit for priesthood. *(Prov. 26: 7; 2 Sam. 5: 8; Lev. 21: 17-23; Job 29: 15; Is. 35: 6)*

Moving: Change in ministry; change in the natural; dissatisfaction with where you are. *(Ez. 12: 3; Gen. 11: 31; 12: 1-3; Acts 7: 2-4)*

Paint: Doctrine, truth or deception.

Painting: Also Drawing: Covering; regenerate; remodel; renovate; love. *(1 Peter 4: 8; Matt. 23: 27; Titus 3: 5; Acts 18: 24)*

Artist's paint: Words; illustrative message; eloquent; humorous; articulate

House painter's brush: Ministry or minister

Playing: Worship; idolatry; covetousness; true worship; spiritual warfare; striving; competition. *(1 Cor. 9: 24; 10: 7; Col. 3: 5)*

Playing an Instrument: Prophesying; worship and praising Him; warring in the Spirit; soothing the soul; worship of self; idolatry; activity or action that proceed from the heart; joy; praise; prophesying; ministry of the gifts of the Spirit; temptation to sin; mesmerized; seduced; words are important to know what the message is; entertainment; teaching; admonishing; edifying. *(Ez. 33: 32; Dan. 3: 5; Is. 5: 1; Jer. 7: 34; 1 Cor. 9: 24; 10: 7; Gen. 31: 27; Matt. 9: 18, 23; Ex. 15: 20-21; 2 Chron. 5: 11-13; Eph. 5: 19; Col. 3: 16; 3: 5)*

R - Z

Raining: God's blessings; God's Word and Spirit outpoured; life; revival; Holy Spirit; trial; disappointment. *(Zech 10: 1; Is. 55: 10-11; Matt. 7: 27; Jer. 3: 3)*

Drought: Blessings withheld because of sin; without God's presence.

Reaping: Fruitfulness for acts; perverse or uprightness deeds being rewarded. *(1 Cor. 9: 11; Prov. 22: 8; Hos. 8: 7; Gal. 6: 8-9; Lev. 26: 5)*

Rending: (as in Garment or Hands): Anger; deep grief; discord and disunity. *(Matt. 7: 6; 9: 16; 26: 65; Luke 5: 36; 1 Sam. 28: 17)*

Resting: Refreshing; ceasing from activity; relaxation; too relaxed; not paying attention; insolent. *(Ps. 132: 8, 14; Is. 11: 10; 14: 63: 14; Matt. 11: 28-30)*

Rocking: Old; past memories; meditation; rest; retirement; prayer. *(Jer. 6: 16)*

Rowing: Work; working out life's problems; earnest prayer; spiritual labor. *(Mark 6: 48; Phil. 2: 30)*

Running: Swiftness; striving; working out one's salvation; faith; haste; trial. *(1 Cor. 9: 24; Jer. 12: 5; Prov. 1: 6; Rev. 9: 9; 1 Cor. 9: 24; Is. 40: 31)*

Singing: See also Song and Music: Rejoicing; thanksgiving; prayer; praise; worship of God or of idols. *(Ps. 7: 17; 9: 2; 13: 6; 18: 49; 21: 13; 27: 6; James 5: 13; Ex. 15: 1; Is. 12: 5; 23: 16-19)*

Sitting: See also Chair and Throne: Power; throne of authority; rulership; Rest; position; concentration; receiving; place of authority; inner court of the temple; throne of God; satanic powers; mercy seat; Kingship of the Lord. *(Rev. 13: 2; Ps. 1: 1; 7: 7; Job 23: 3; 2 Chron. 9: 18; 19: 8; Matt. 17: 19; Heb. 9: 5-12; Ex. 25: 22; 29: 42-43; 1 John 2: 2; Num. 7: 89; Rom. 3: 24-25; 2 Cor. 5: 20; 1 Tim. 2: 5)*

Skiing: Faith; support by God's power through faith; fast progress. *(John 6: 19-21; Matt. 14: 29-31)*

Sleeping: Indifference; death; rest; unconscience; unaware (hidden or covered); ignorant; danger; laziness; refreshing; spiritual stupor; indifference. *(Is. 29: 10; Rom. 13: 11; Ps. 127: 2; Prov. 20: 13)*

Overslept: Danger of missing a divine appointment.

Smiling: Friendly; kindness; benevolent; good will; without offense; seduction. *(Prov. 18: 24)*

Sowing: Dispersing seed; seed can be righteous or evil. *(Gal. 6: 7-8; 2 Cor. 9: 6; Job 4: 8; Ps. 126: 5; Matt. 13: 3-9; 11-33; 37-53; Mark 4: 1-20; Luke 13: 18-19)*

Speaking: See Tongue, Voice and Arrows: Thunder; compelling; words of Christ; indication to open the door of our heats to receive Jesus; sound of many waters; but sheep know HIS voice; sign of a covenant; requires obedience; important to test the spirit by the Word; language; speech; can be used for good or evil; blessings; cursing; something only God can tame; life and death in it's power; can start a fire for good or evil. *(Zech. 9:7-8; Is. 7: 16; Rom. 5: 3-4; Col. 2: 8; 1 Tim. 6: 20; Prov. 25: 18-19; Ez. 18: 2; Ps. 11: 2; 45: 5; 64: 3; 76: 3; 91: 5; 119: 9; 127: 4; Jer. 9: 8; Job 6: 4; Du. 32: 23, 42; John 4: 1; 10: 4; Heb. 5: 8; 12: 26; Rev. 1: 15; 3: 20; Is. 66: 6; Matt. 3: 3; Josh 24: 24-25; Gen. 3: 1-19; 22: 6-18; 1)*

Sprinkling: Washing for cleansing; consecrating. *(1 Peter 1: 2; Lev. 1: 5-11; 14: 7; Heb. 9: 13)*

Standing: Incomplete task; virtue; standing on or committed to a point of view or belief. *(Acts 7: 55-56; Heb. 10: 11; Eph. 6: 13)*

Straight: Sitting, Standing or Walking: Going in the right direction; not crooked spiritually; unyielding. *(Heb. 12: 13; Matt. 3: 3; Ps. 5: 8; Luke 3: 4-5)*

Stumbling: Barrier in the way preventing the truth; sin; backslide; mistake; become deceived; to be overcome; ignorance. *(Jer. 50: 32; Rom. 11: 9; Is. 5: 24; Ex. 15: 7; 1 Cor. 1: 23; 8: 9; 1 Peter 2: 8; Prov. 3: 23)*

Suicide: Self destructive; self hatred; grief; remorse; foolish action. *(Ecc. 7: 16; Matt. 27: 5)*

Sweating: The effort of man; fleshly works; striving in the flesh. *(Gen. 3: 19; Luke 22: 44)*

Sweeping: Cleaning house (own tent, tabernacle that the Holy Spirit lives in); repentance; change; actively taking barriers down; admonishment of sinners. *(Is. 28: 17; Eph. 4: 31; 2 Cor. 7: 1; 2 Cor. 7: 11; 1 Tim. 5: 20)*

Swimming: Conducting spiritual activity; worship; gifts of the Spirit being applied; service to God; prophecy in operation. *(Ez. 47: 5; Eph. 3: 8)*

Swimming Pool: Spiritual place or condition; church; home; family; God's blessings.

Dirty or Dry: Corrupt or destitute spiritual condition; backslide.

Swinging: Peaceful; rest; quietness; romance; fellowship. *(Is. 30: 15)*

Swinging High: Danger; thrill seeking; immorality; infidelity.

Tasting: Experience; discern; try; test; judge. *(Ps. 34: 8; 119: 103; Heb. 2: 9; 6: 4; Ex. 16: 31; John 2: 9; Matt. 27:*

34)

Upward Motion: Also see Tower, Mountain, Hill, Skyscraper, and Elevator: Prophetic church of great revelation; high places; above earthly experience; higher spiritual things; spiritual ascension; pride; self exaltation; strength; protection; safety; Tower of Babel; dominance; control; obstacle; Jesus returning from the heavens to earth; symbolic of victory; Jesus being lifted up on the cross; wisdom that comes from above; Mt. Zion; sacrifice of worship; Mt. Sinai and the Ark of the Covenant in the Temple; Songs of ascent unto Him; Mt. Carmel; Beatitudes in the Sermon on the Mount. *(Acts 1: 13-14; 20: 7-8; Ps. 61: 3; 103: 11; 144: 2; 1 Sam. 9: 12-14; Matt 5; 1 Kings 18; John 3: 7; James 3: 15, 17; Heb. 1: 3; 1 Thess. 4: 13-18; 1 Kings 12: 31; Prov. 18: 19; Is. 30: 25)*

Urinating: If full, pressure; compelling urge; temptation, repentance; if infection or cancer: offense or enmity. *(Prov. 17: 14; 1 Sam. 25: 22)*

Walking: Progress; living in the Spirit; living in sin; the conduct of the dreamer or their lifestyle and actions. *(Gal. 5: 16-25; Eph. 4: 17; 1 John 1: 6-7; 2 Cor. 5: 7)*

Difficult walking: Trials; opposition.

Warring: Total destruction; death; great ruin; prayer and worship; final war in heaven and in earth. *(Rev. 12: 7-17; 17: 14; 19: 11-19; 1 Peter 2: 11; 1 Tim. 1: 18; James 4: 1-2; 2 Cor. 10: 3; Eph. 6: 10-18; 2 Chron. 20)*

Washing: Cleansing from sin and the filth of this world. *(John 9: 7; 13: 5-14; Lev. 1: 13-19)*

Wind Blowing: See also Clouds, Thunder, Tornado, Storm and Whirlwind: Powers of God or satan; breathe of life; spirit or doctrine; Holy Spirit; demonic or strong opposition; empty words such as boasting; vanity; calamity; God's adjudication and correction and quota or portion; demise and failure of man; false teaching. *(Eph. 4: 14; John 3: 8; Acts 2: 2-4; Job 1: 12, 19; 8: 2; Prov. 25: 14; Ez. : 10; Eph. 4: 14; Is. 32: 2; Hos. 8: 7; 13: 15)*

Wrestling: Striving; deliverance; resistance; persistence; trial; tribulation; controlling spirit (in a **person**); attempting to gain control. *(Gen. 32: 24-28; Eph. 6: 12; 2 Tim. 2: 24)*

ABOUT THE AUTHOR

Dr. Ricardo Vincent is the Founder of "Global Prophetic Ministries" a ministry whose drive is to facilitate and develop the giftings and growth of believers within the body. He has been in ministry for over 30 years. He was one who pioneered the School of Prophetic Ministry in 1996 in Trinidad and Tobago. He has three (3) radio programs on two (2) local radio stations. He has also conducted several workshops, internationally. He and his wife Kathleen are involved in ministry together and they are the parent of two lovely sons.

For speaking engagements or counseling, you can contact Dr. Ricardo Vincent at:

Global Prophetic Ministries
P.O. Box 12
San Fernando
Trinidad, West Indies
Email: rvincent@consultant.com
Ph. No: (868) 379 - 6813

4505169

Made in the USA
Lexington, KY
01 February 2010